CONTEMPORARY STENCILS

CONTEMPORARY STENCILS

MAGIE M. MAULE

Angus&Robertson
An imprint of HarperCollins*Publishers*

An Angus & Robertson Publication

Angus&Robertson, an imprint of
HarperCollins *Publishers*
25 Ryde Road, Pymble, Sydney NSW 2073, Australia
31 View Road, Glenfield, Auckland 10, New Zealand

First published in Australia in 1994

National Library of Australia
Cataloguing-in-Publication data:

Maule, Magie, M.
        Contemporary Stencils

        ISBN 0 207 18291 4
        1. Stencil work. I. Title.

745.73

Printed in Hong Kong
Illustrations by Magie Maule

9 8 7 6 5 4 3 2 1
97 96 95 94

CONTENTS

PREFACE

Stencilling seems to be even more popular now than when I began designing my first stencil books. I hope that my efforts have helped in some small way to create this increased interest.

Contemporary Stencils is my sixth stencil design book. This time I thought it would be nice to break with tradition and look to stencilling in the future, so I have created more than 100 contemporary designs for modern homes, textiles and furniture. I have done this with the hope of involving a whole new generation of stencillers and home decorators in the creative and exciting world of stencilling. After all, each generation should make its own artistic contribution instead of always looking to the past for motifs. Therefore, I have included all sorts of useful motifs and borders that will suit the most modern homes.

Stencilling has endless possibilities — with this skill you will be able to transform your home, making rooms artistic and unique in a world of mass-produced products. There is real scope for creativity and play with this interesting art form, altering designs and combinations to suit yourself — and it will all be your own handiwork.

MAGIE M. MAULE

INTRODUCTION

A DEFINITION OF STENCILLING

A stencil can be a piece of cardboard (stencil board), plastic (mylar) or metal (usually brass) into which you cut holes to form a design. Paint is then brushed or sprayed through these holes to create the decorative pattern. The holes are held together by bridges or ties of material. The ties are arranged to make the stencil strong and also to outline or highlight the design. A good stencil design integrates the ties so that they accentuate and enhance the motif. You can use one stencil to make as many repeats of the design as you wish, so for the amount of initial effort required in cutting your stencil you are rewarded by being able to decorate large areas very quickly.

HOW TO USE THE STENCILS IN THIS BOOK

The stencils in this book simply need to be photocopied to the size you require. If you reduce them in size you will find that the ties or bridges between the holes of some designs become very thin and break. You will need to increase the width of the bridges to strengthen them by going over them with white correction fluid (liquid paper).

CUTTING YOUR STENCIL

MATERIALS

- One piece of drafting film/mylar/overhead projection film that is 1 inch (2.5 cm) larger all round than your design
- Sticky tape
- One small, sharp cutter or surgeon's scalpel or a small pair of nail scissors
- One cutting board (you can use a thick cardboard, a self-healing cutting mat or a sheet of glass with cut edges bound with insulating tape for safety)

Stick the drafting film on top of the photocopied design with tape. This is so that the two can be moved as one if you need to swivel the design around the blade to cut smoother curves and circles. You can use stencil board, acrylic sheet or overhead projection film instead of drafting film. If you are using overhead projection film you can photocopy the design onto it, so you won't need to stick the film and the design together. You should cut the stencil on a cutting board.

If your cutter slips when you are working, don't worry. You can easily repair the damage with sticky tape stuck down firmly on both sides of the stencil. (This will have to be replaced from time to time if you use oil-based paint and clean the stencil with turpentine (turps). It helps if you hold your cutting blade at an angle of 45 degrees to the cutting board. Work from the smallest areas to the largest. Take care at sharp corners.

Small circles and holes are difficultto cut out. Practise them by gently swivelling the stencil sheet around the tip of the cutting blade, rather than moving the blade edge in a circle. It is also possible to buy cutting blades with swivelling edges. These are very useful once you have practised with them.

When all the areas of the design have been cut out, your stencil is finished and ready for stencilling.

STENCILLING

You can hold your stencil in place on walls and floors with sticky tape. You can also sticky tape your stencil onto fabrics and furniture, but I much prefer to stick mine down with contact adhesive spray. If it is used properly the adhesive lessens the chance of pulling background paint off the wall or floor.

The contact adhesive should be sprayed lightly over the back of your stencil. **This should be done out of doors because you must not inhale the spray.** Follow the manufacturer's instructions concerning the amount of time it needs to dry. Do not stick the stencil down when it is wet or you will end up with a nasty clean-up job ahead of you with a rubber.

APPLYING YOUR STENCIL

You can colour your stencil with paint (oil or acrylic), oil crayons or spray cans, and you have the choice of applying it with brushes, rollers or sponges.

PAINT

In my business of interior decorating we use a lot of oil paint — to achieve complex painted effects and to stencil. I like using oil paint for stencilling because of its intense colours and its traditional 'artist palette'. You can mix and match any colours with oil paint. It has a vitality that seems to be lacking in acrylic paint. Acrylic paint is improving, though, and there is an excellent range of colours now available. Acrylic paints dry quickly and are waterproof when dry — just like oils.

You should buy artist tubes or Flat Japan oil paint, available from sign-writer suppliers. Flat oil paint is good because it dries very quickly. When using oil paint, mix it with a little turps in an old saucer until it becomes thin and creamy. If you are using more than 250 ml, strain the paint through an old nylon stocking. This is particularly important if the paint is from a pot or can that has previously been opened, because paint brushes transfer dirt and grit to the paint.

SPRAY CANS

It is better to use a spray can when you are stencilling metallic colours. This is because spray can paint gives a gleaming, shiny surface which is uninterrupted by brush marks and stippling. It also dries very quickly. When using spray can paint you must 'mask' the area above and below your spray line with newspaper because the spray can drift much further than you think. Some stencillers use nothing but sprays and mix the colours together on the stencil to give lovely, soft effects. Always wear a proper industrial mask when spraying. A 'dust' mask is not good enough.

STENCILLING CRAYONS

Stencilling crayons are rather like lipsticks with a protective varnish coat to prevent them drying out. They are much softer than the traditional oil pastel crayons. **They should not be rubbed through the stencil** but scribbled on a piece of card and carefully transferred to the stencil with a stencil brush.

STENCILS BRUSHES

If you are doing a lot of stencilling you will need stencil brushes of different sizes. Stencil brushes are cylindrical and have bristles that are cut off straight across the top (not tapered like an ordinary paint brush). They are usually made of hog's hair. You will need one brush for each colour you use in any one session because you can't wash stencil brushes out with turps (for oil paint) or water (for acrylics). If you did this you would dilute the next batch of colour you use and get blots around your stencil. You should just clean your brush periodically by wiping it off on a piece of clean rag.

Stencilling with a stencil brush is not like conventional painting, where the brush is moved from side to side and up and down. A stencil brush is held like a pen between the thumb, index and second finger. The flat cut-off bristles on a stencil brush should be held parallel to the printing surface and the painting motion you should use is called 'pouncing'. This is done by tapping through the stencil with the paint laden brush, lifting it off each time. Tap from the edges to the centre, gradually building up the colour density. You may shade colours as you go and blend in other colours.

Once your paint is mixed you can practise your first stencil on paper. Dip your brush lightly into the paint taking up a small amount. Tap the brush out onto a piece of

newspaper and work the paint evenly into the bristles until very little paint is left. Then start pouncing through the stencil. This way you avoid blots, get a crisp edge and the paint dries quickly. If you have too little paint on your brush you can increase it. It is much better to have too little paint than too much.

ROLLERS

You can buy tiny sponge rollers from hardware shops that are ideal for applying paint onto stencils. They make slow jobs fast and are even good on fabric. To use them you simply dip your roller into the prepared paint (see page 8) and then very gently roll it out on newspaper and dip it back into the paint until the roller is lightly covered. Roll on the stencil from outer edges to centre of the holes. Again, be very careful not to overload your roller with paint.

SPONGES

Paint can also be applied with a sea or synthetic sponge. This will achieve a full colour coverage or a textured 'sponged' effect that can be very attractive. To apply paint this way, dip the sponge gently into the paint and tap it out onto a piece of newspaper until the sponge is full of paint (not saturated or dripping). Tap the coated sponge gently through the stencil until a full coat of colour is obtained (unless you prefer a mottled effect, which can look abandoned and spontaneous).

STENCILLING ON DIFFERENT SURFACES

You should always prepare a surface before you begin stencilling onto it. Hard surfaces should be repaired, filled, sanded, made smooth or washed down before you begin stencilling. Soft surfaces like fabric or paper should be smoothed out and stuck down using a contact adhesive (in the case of fabric) or removable tape (in the case of paper). New fabric should be washed first to remove the dressing and to see if it shrinks. It should then be ironed before you start to stencil.

MATERIALS

- Oil paint/water paint/stencilling crayons
- Stencil brushes (small, medium or large depending on the work involved), rollers, sponges
- Spray adhesive and solvent
- Chalk, chalk-liners and a plumb bob for walls
- Set square
- Pencil
- Masking tape/low tack (not very sticky) tape or stencillers' tape
- Newspaper
- Old rags
- Old saucer or plate
- Turpentine
- Sheet of drawing paper
- Scissors

WALLS

When stencilling walls, you will probably be stencilling repeating borders, spot designs (where motifs are regularly placed but not connected), or a repeating, all-over design. Whichever pattern you choose, use chalk when you map out the structure of the design, because it can be rubbed off easily afterwards.

First, use a plumb bob to establish your true uprights (straight vertical lines). The plumb bob string should be covered with chalk by running chalk up and down the string until it is well coated. Hang it from the ceiling and let it swing until it comes to rest. Hold the string of the bob at the top and bottom against the wall (you will need two people for this), then pull out the string in the middle towards you, like plucking a guitar string, and let it flick against the wall. It will leave a perfectly straight chalk line from which you can measure all other vertical and horizontal lines using a set square. From this you can map out the geometric structure that you require for your design. For an all-over repeating design you should map out the stencil so that you know where every piece of it falls — the squares, diamonds, bands and whatever else it includes.

If you are making a repeated border out of stencils you will need to know where the second, third and subsequent placements fall. You will need to measure these. Tracing film, which is semi-transparent, makes judging the placings quite easy. Just place your stencil next to the original design. Decide what space there will be between them and make marks on three places on the tracing film. When you make the next stencil design you will always place these marks in the same spot in relation to the previous print. Try this system on clean paper before you start on walls.

On stencil board that is not transparent, punch out small holes that you can see through, or use nicks in the edge of the stencil, so that you always get the same piece of the previous stencil showing through the hole.

Allow each placement of the stencil to dry before putting the stencil down again otherwise you'll pick up paint on the underside of your stencil and transfer it to the wall. If this happens, remove the marks. Make sure you wipe the wall and the back of the stencil. Use turps (for oil paint and stencilling crayons), and allow the turps to dry before you try again. Remove acrylic paint marks from the wall with water or methylated spirits. To prevent a mistake turning into a disaster, make sure your wall is painted with low sheen acrylic. Oil paint will come off an acrylic surface easily with turps. So will acrylic paint, using water — but you have to be quick. Don't use methylated spirits on newly-painted acrylic walls — the background paint will come off as well as your mistake!

To stencil walls, stick your stencil to the wall with spray adhesive. The adhesive lasts for 10 to 12 placings before you need to spray it again. Build up can be removed by placing the stencil (clean side down) on an old towel and rubbing it with a turps rag. Build up of paint on the front of the stencil must be removed with the appropriate solvent (methylated spirits or turps). The sticky back of your stencil must be put down on a piece of clean plastic or other dust-free surface, otherwise dirt from that area could be transferred to the wall.

If you think your stencilled wall design will be in for some wear and tear add a little oil-based varnish to your oil paint, or water-based varnish to your acrylic paint.

Some of the stencils in this book have been designed so that separate shapes must be cut for each separate colour and placed accordingly, but most only need single cuttings. You can still use more than one colour on these by simply covering up with tape any bits you don't want painted in. Remove tape when you want to fill the spaces with a second or third colour. Do not remove the stencil from the wall until all the colours you want have been put in place.

WOODEN FLOORS

Floors need a little more explanation than walls, but they are easier to stencil than walls or ceilings as you have both hands free (you are not up a ladder). Floors should be sanded smooth — by a professional sander if possible — who will also hammer in all loose nails and fill in nail head holes and other defects. The floor should be given two good oil-based undercoats after it has been thoroughly vacuumed and gone over with a tack rag (which you can buy from a hardware shop). A tack rag is a cloth that is made sticky by impregnated varnish and linseed oil. It will pick up dust and dirt from any surface that you have sanded. It is an invaluable piece of equipment.

Each undercoat of paint will take 24 to 48 hours to dry, so the room should be locked, or closed off in some other way, to avoid cats, dogs and children (and adults!) leaving little traces. Undercoating should be followed by at least two coats (also oil-based) of your chosen background colour. You can buy special fast-drying floor paints that are excellent. If you follow all these instructions you will have a good surface to work on. One last vacuum and thorough going over with your tack rag and you are ready to stencil.

If you are making a repeating design on a floor, lay out your work using chalked string the same way as for a wall. If you are using a diamond or chequerboard design, two lines taken from the corners and crossing in the middle will give you the centre.

When painting the floor there are two golden rules:

1. Cover your hair completely as some hairs always drop into the wet paint. (If you find hairs on the floor while it is still wet, you can remove them. Wrap sticky tape around your index finger and then dab your finger on the floor lightly.)

2. Don't get trapped! Start in the far corner and paint your way out of the room towards the door. If the floor is made of boards, paint along the line of the floor boards. Your main coats of paint can be applied with a roller on the end of a long pole to avoid the backbreaking job of brush painting. If you are putting down another covering in sections (craft board for example) these can be undercoated before laying.

When your design is finished and completely dry you will need to varnish it. Five coats of Polyurethane Satin Varnish give a good wearing surface. You will need to sand lightly after each coat is dry, then vacuum and use the tack rag. Make sure you follow the directions on the can and allow the correct drying time. You should now have a hard-wearing floor that can be simply mopped clean with a damp sponge. If the surface starts to wear, give it a light sanding and apply a few more coats of varnish.

It is particularly important to strain paint and varnish, because cans always end up with bits of dirt and grit in them; they are transferred from the floor to the brush no matter how carefully you have cleaned and dusted the floor.

FURNITURE

Furniture that you are planning to stencil should be in sound condition, so repair where necessary. Fill all the holes and sand in between (whether the furniture piece is painted or clean wood) till it is smooth all over. Preparation is the most important part of a well-painted piece of furniture.

Use two oil-based coats of undercoat, then two thin coats of your main colour. Don't overload your brush, or you will get a dribble. If you do, rub it flat (if it's wet), or remove it with a scalpel, then sand smooth. Using water, sand lightly between the colour coats with fine 'wet and dry' using a circular motion. Clean off the 'mud' that appears with hot soapy water, then dry the area thoroughly. When it is quite dry, begin stencilling. First, apply a thin coat of white French Polish, with a clean rag, all over the paint surface. This acts as a barrier between the colour coat and the stencil coat — if you make a mistake it can be wiped off with turps. Choose a stencil design to suit the style of the piece of furniture and make sure it is in good proportion to the size of the surface on which you are working.

Once your stencilling is dry (it can take up to 48 hours) protect it with several coats of matt, satin or gloss varnish, whichever is appropriate to the appearance of the piece. I recommend three to five coats, lightly sanded with 'wet and dry' between coats. This will ensure you end up with a piece of furniture which is silky smooth to the touch. It can be further protected with wax polish.

FABRIC

Stencilling on fabric is essentially the same as for the surfaces already described, but there are a few differences.

MATERIALS

- Stencil, preferably made out of drafting film
- Clean butcher's paper (not newsprint — it will leave dirty marks)

- ◆ Spray adhesive
- ◆ Fabric dyes or paints
- ◆ Stencil brushes and sponge rollers
- ◆ Drawing boards or a flat printing table
- ◆ Drawing pins
- ◆ Fabric

If you are using stencil board you will have to waterproof your stencil by giving it several coats of metallic spray paint on both sides, because fabric dyes and paints are water soluble and will make the board disintegrate. If you use an acrylic or plastic stencil it will already be waterproof.

New fabric should be washed to remove any dressing and then ironed and pinned out flat or stuck down with spray adhesive. Fabric or garments should be pinned or taped firmly to a hard, flat surface on top of several layers of butcher's paper, which absorbs excess dye or paint and reduces blotching. Remember to put paper inside the garments as well, otherwise you will have two printed layers — front and back!

Stencil with your brush as for the oil paint method and leave to dry or paint your dye onto the fabric with a small sponge roller (this is a very fast neat method which gives even coverage). Treat according to the instructions on the fabric paint. After stencilling, lampshades, curtains and blinds can be sprayed with 'Scotchguard' water-proofer to protect them.

You might also like to stencil a design onto tapestry canvas and embroider as usual. This way you can create entire room schemes around stencilled themes.

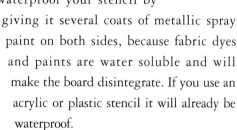

There are so many things you can make out of stencils on paper — lampshades, book covers, cards, stationery and even drawer liners. Try stencilling on some of the lovely rag papers available, or vellum or Japanese handmade papers. Try making your own wallpaper by printing on rolls of lining paper.

MATERIALS

- ◆ Stencil brushes
- ◆ Artists' watercolours, gouache colours, poster colour or ink
- ◆ Any kind of absorbent paper, parchment or vellum
- ◆ Metallic spray paint

For this stencilling use the brush (as for previous methods), or matt paint from a can, or ink (using a mouth spray). Before you begin stencilling, waterproof your stencil (if it is off stencil board) by spraying both sides of it with several layers of metallic paint. Pin out the sheets of paper, or tape the extreme edges, onto the clean floor (or a long table). Pad underneath with newsprint.

Secure your stencils with spray adhesive but first make sure the surface is dry (try a piece on the paper first — it may fluff the paper's surface when you pull it off). Then stencil in the usual way, with a brush or a sponge roller. Hold your brush like a pen and use the pouncing technique described earlier, with very little paint. Your work can be protected with a spray of clear varnish that is especially designed to make paper moisture-proof and dirt-proof ('Dean's Crystal Varnish' is ideal).

If you want to stencil a lampshade it is best to find some good quality card, parchment or vellum and cut it to shape, stencilling while flat and assembling the shade later. Ready-made lampshades can be stencilled with spray paint, using plenty of masking tape, or with coloured ink and an artists' mouth spray (again masking surrounding areas well). Protect your

design with clear paper varnish and it will wipe clean. You can also make lampshades without paint by cutting the shade out like a large stencil and lining it inside with different coloured paper or cloth. This gives an interesting effect when the light shines through.

EXISTING TILES

MATERIALS

- ESP (a preparation that makes oil paint stick better)
- Oil paint
- Liquid latex (if you want to retain the grout lines)
- Turps (to fix spills and retain grout lines)
- Satin Polyurethane Finish Varnish

If you have attractive old titles in your kitchen or bathrooms please do not stencil them. This applies especially to Australian tiles made between the World Wars that are often sponged or spotched with lovely colours and have lovely bands and arrangements. But if you have been left with awful 1950s, 1960s and 1970s tiles you will want to do something about them. Brown/orange, lime green/yellow and red/black tiles are very difficult to live with but you can solve the problem by painting and stencilling them.

First, cover the offending tiles with ESP (follow the directions on the can), then apply thin coats of oil paint (in the colour of your choice). ESP doesn't work with water-based paints. If you want to retain the original grout colour paint the grout lines with liquid latex. The latex

can be peeled off as soon as you have finished painting; make sure you do this before the paint dries. Another way of retaining the grout lines is to go over them with a cotton wool bud that is soaked in turpentine after you've painted all over them.

You can decorate the painted tiles with painted finishes (ragging, sponging etc.), and you can stencil on top of this finish with more oil paint. After you have completed your design, make sure that the grout lines are clear, then cover the tiles with a polyurethane satin finish varnish. You should use five coats if these tiles are in 'wet' areas of the house.

TERRACOTTA TILES

MATERIALS

- Oil paint
- Sealer
- Tack rag

You should stencil terracotta tiles before you seal them. When stencilling these tiles always use oil paint and when you seal them use several coats of sealer. If you use a water-based sealer, the stencilling should be done in a water-based paint. Terracotta floor tiles are bound to get a lot of traffic and therefore wear quickly. This is another reason for using many coats of sealer.

LINO FLOORS

MATERIALS

- Matt oil paint
- Satin (or matt) polyurethane varnish

These may be stencilled in any way with oil paint (matt oil paint is preferable). They should then be sealed with matt or satin polyurethane varnish.

VINYL FLOORS

MATERIALS

- Permanent markers (the sort used to mark freezer bags)
- Vinyl floor sealer and polisher

Vinyl cannot be painted with ordinary paint but it will take permanent marker pens — the ones that won't rub off, as the mother of any small child will tell you! Mark out your stencils with permanent markers by drawing around the holes then systematically filling in the shapes. This takes a long time and many pens, so be patient. When the design is finished seal it with a vinyl floor sealer and polisher. The problem with using permanent markers is that you are limited in colour to black, blue and red. A light background is best to show up these colours.

If you are 'faux' tiling plank floor boards, the width of the plank dictates the tile dimensions and you only need to have 'grout' lines across the tiles. You can make these with a grey fibre-tipped pen or the chosen background before stencilling begins. Small drop-in diamonds between octagonal tiles can be stencilled in batches of six using a large stencil and spray can paint — take care, however, because some sprays act like paint stripper on oil paints. Your finished stencil design will need five coats of satin polyurethane varnish — more if you use matt, as it isn't so hard-wearing. Polish the final result with good quality beeswax if you like, but if you need to 'patch' the wear areas later, the polish must be carefully removed before re-varnishing.

MAKING 'FAUX' TILED FLOORS

MATERIALS

- Chalk
- Graphic tape or liquid latex
- Grey fibre-tipped pen
- Satin or matt polyurethane varnish
- Beeswax

These are best painted on wooden plank floors because the series of parallel lines make the work easy. If you are working on a composite floor you will have to measure out a grid on the floor using chalk lines. Use a ruler to go over the chalk lines with fine graphic tape or liquid latex applied with a fine brush.

CERAMICS AND GLASS

Glazed ceramics, such as lamp bases, can be stencilled — use the same instructions as for 'Existing Tiles'. Glass can also be treated in the same way, though it won't be very hard-wearing.

FORMICA WORKBENCHES

These can also be painted and stencilled as for 'Ceramics and Glass', but they must be meticulously sealed with many coats of varnish (sanded between coats) and, of course, you can't cut or chop on the surface. If they are treated like marble they will last for years.

LIST OF STOCKISTS

NEW SOUTH WALES

Janet's Art Supplies
145 Victoria Avenue
Chatswood NSW 2067
Ph: (02) 417 8572
Fax: (02) 417 7617

Deans Art
21 Atchison Street
St Leonards NSW 2065
Ph: (02) 439 4944
Fax: (02) 906 1632

VICTORIA

The Stencil House
662 Glenferrie Road
Hawthorn Vic 3122
Ph: (03) 819 0421
Fax: (03) 819 0467

SOUTH AUSTRALIA

Premier Art Supplies
43 Gilles Street
Adelaide SA 5000
Ph: (08) 212 5922

WESTERN AUSTRALIA

Jackson's Drawing
Supplies
103 Rokeby Road
Subiaco WA 6008
Ph: (09) 381 2488

TASMANIA

Artery
137–141 Collins Street
Hobart 7000
Ph: (002) 343 788

SANTA FE STYLE

THESE DESIGNS HAVE THAT POPULAR SOUTH-OF-THE-BORDER LOOK, BRINGING THE OPEN SPACES AND CLEAR SKIES OF THE DESERT INTO YOUR HOME. THERE ARE DESERT CREATURES (LIZARDS, BIRDS, ANTELOPE, LLAMA, A DOG), PLANTS, AND EVEN A BUFFALO SKULL, ALL OF WHICH HAVE SOMETHING NATIVE AMERICAN IN THEIR STYLE. THESE ARE STRONG, SURE DESIGNS, ALL WITH A CLOSENESS TO NATURE AND THE EARTH. THEY WORK BEST IN THE COLOURS OF THE DESERT — TERRACOTTA, SAND, CACTUS GREEN, SKY BLUE. PERFECT FOR FAMILY ROOMS, PATIOS AND COUNTRY SHACKS.

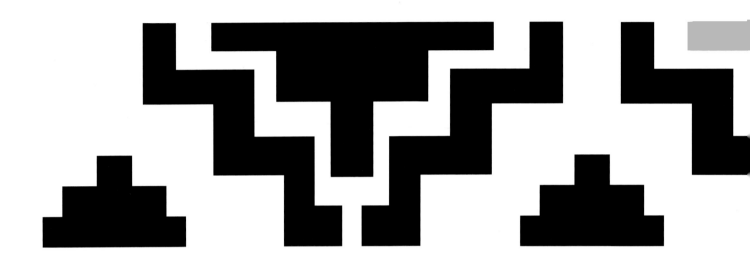

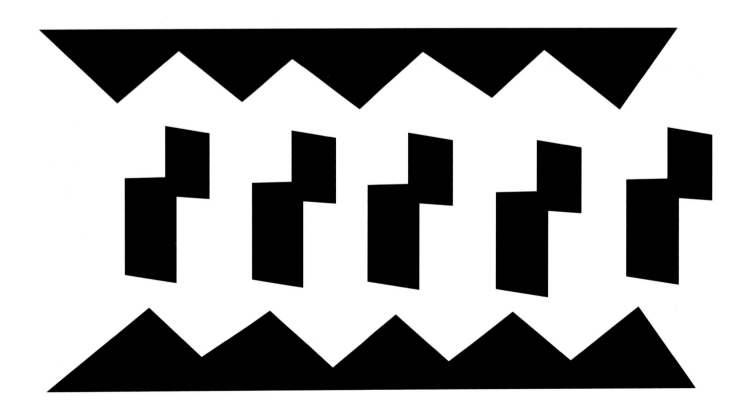

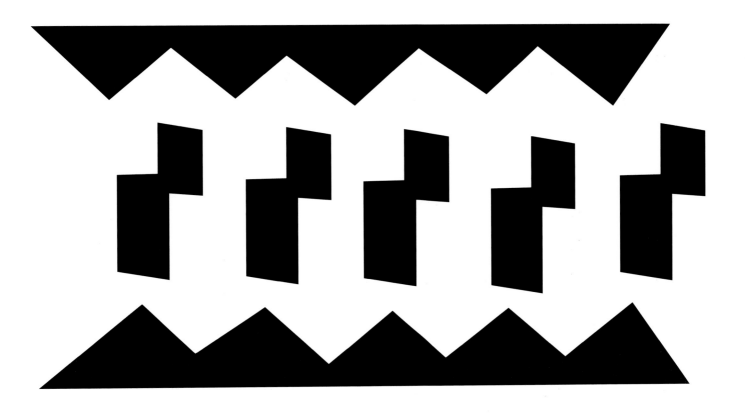

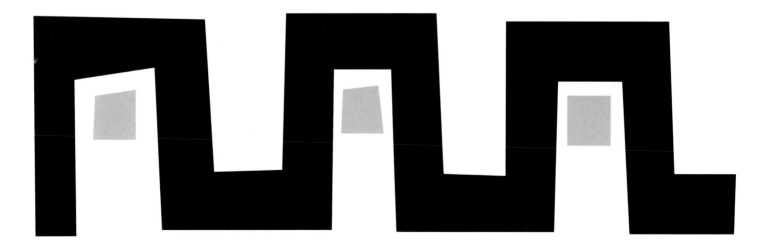

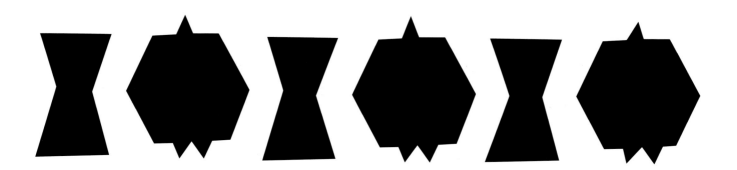

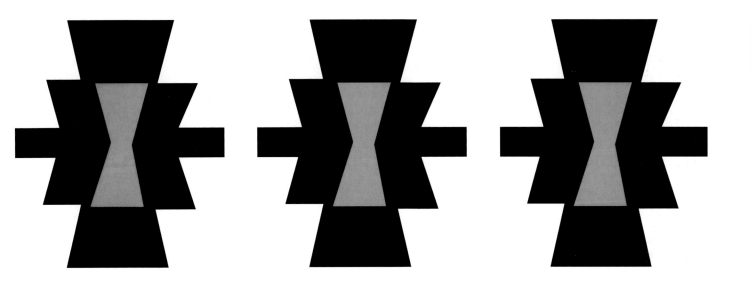

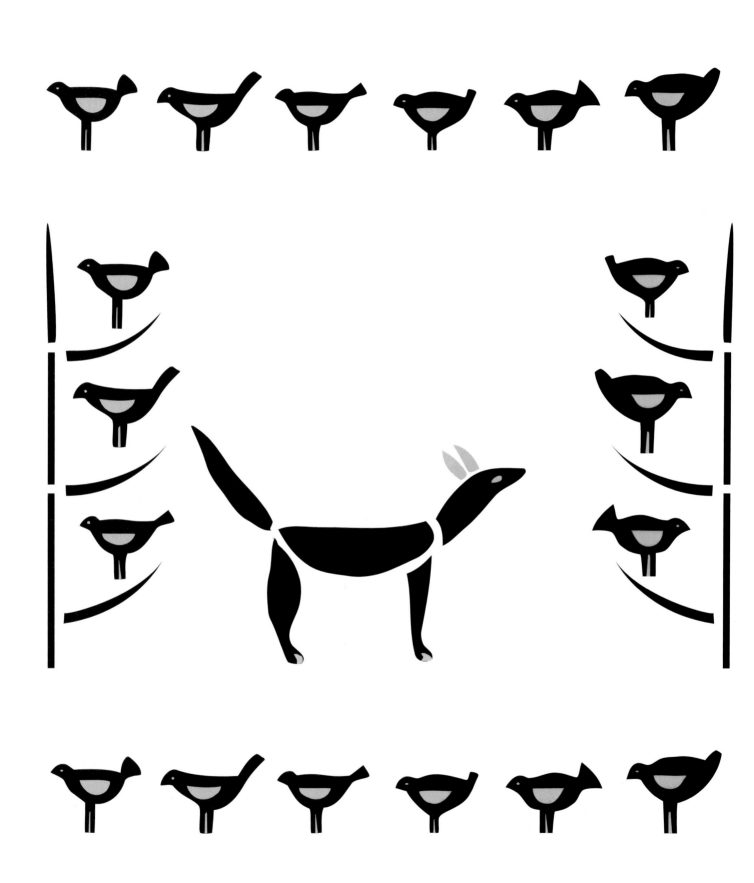

FREEFORM DESIGNS

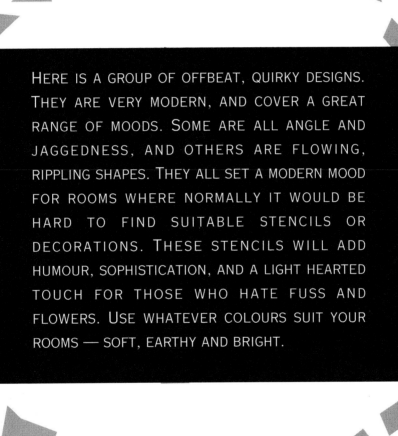

HERE IS A GROUP OF OFFBEAT, QUIRKY DESIGNS. THEY ARE VERY MODERN, AND COVER A GREAT RANGE OF MOODS. SOME ARE ALL ANGLE AND JAGGEDNESS, AND OTHERS ARE FLOWING, RIPPLING SHAPES. THEY ALL SET A MODERN MOOD FOR ROOMS WHERE NORMALLY IT WOULD BE HARD TO FIND SUITABLE STENCILS OR DECORATIONS. THESE STENCILS WILL ADD HUMOUR, SOPHISTICATION, AND A LIGHT HEARTED TOUCH FOR THOSE WHO HATE FUSS AND FLOWERS. USE WHATEVER COLOURS SUIT YOUR ROOMS — SOFT, EARTHY AND BRIGHT.

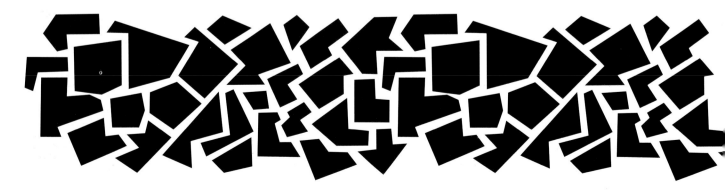

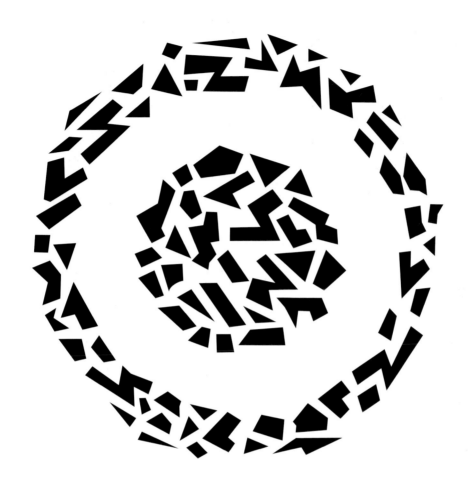

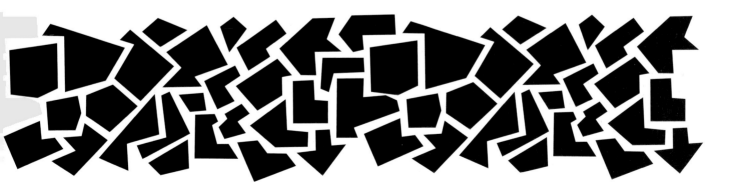

FREEFORM DESIGNS

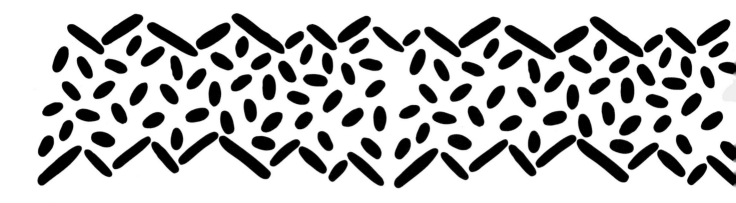

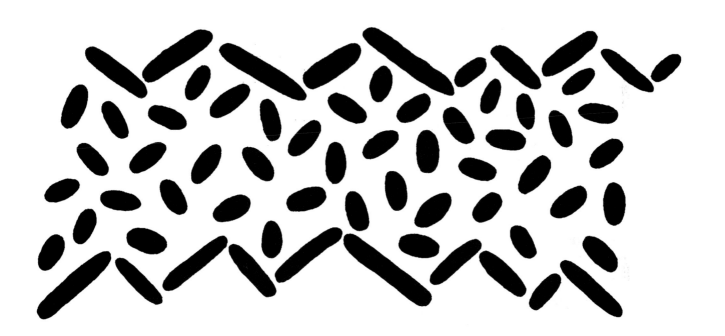

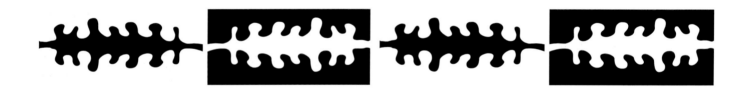

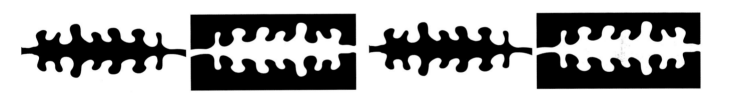

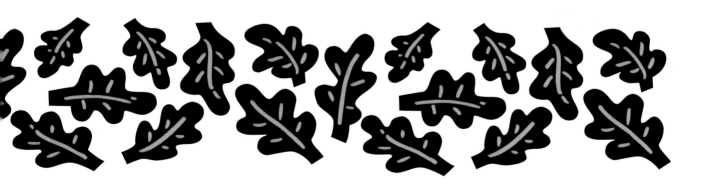

NATURE MOTIFS

THESE DESIGNS PROVIDE WAYS OF BRINGING THE LIFE AND VITALITY OF THE NATURAL WORLD INTO YOUR HOME, BUT IN A NEW AND MODERN WAY. THEY HAVE A FEELING OF SPRING IN THEM, OF GROWTH AND ABUNDANCE. THERE ARE LEAVES, FRUIT AND FLOWERS, AND THERE ARE BIRDS AND INSECTS. SOME ARE HUMOROUS, WITH A LIGHT HEARTED SENSE OF ENERGY AND ENTHUSIASM, WHILE OTHERS ARE STYLISED, SO THERE IS SOMETHING HERE FOR EVERY TASTE. AS WITH ALL THE OTHER GROUPS, THERE IS A MIXTURE OF BORDER DESIGNS, TILE DESIGNS AND INDIVIDUAL IMAGES, SO YOU CAN MIX AND MATCH. THE COLOURS OF THE GARDEN WOULD SUIT THESE IMAGES WELL — A VARIETY OF GREENS FOR THE PLANTS, AND BRIGHT COLOURS FOR THE FLOWERS AND INSECTS. THESE ARE NEW VARIATIONS ON THE COUNTRY THEMES OF HE PAST, PERFECT FOR FLOORS, BEDROOMS, QUILTS, CURTAINS, WALLS TRUNKS AND FURNITURE.

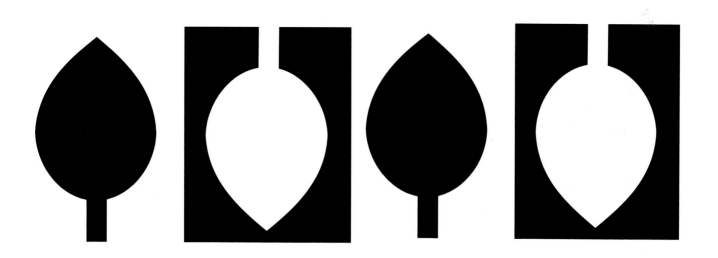

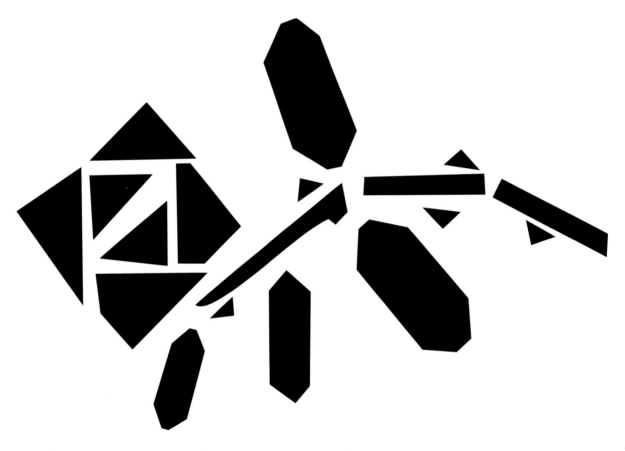

TRIBAL DESIGNS

This group of stencils is full of strong, striking images. There are bold geometric patterns and delicate animal motifs, all of which display a solidity and strength beneath the surface. They are reminders of older cultures, where designs were clearer and simpler. The beauty of these tribal designs is their flexibility — they are strong enough to stand out and enhance any room, in any colour. Pastel colours probably would not suit them, unless reversed out against a dark background, because these designs are not going to be light and frilly edges to your room — they will be outstanding, powerful features, and should be reproduced in bold colours. If you like strength plus sophisticated simplicity, these designs will make your dullest room come instantly alive. Try decorating walls, sofa cushions and lino, table tops, boxes, fabric and paper — even curtains and bed covers.

TRIBAL MOTIFS

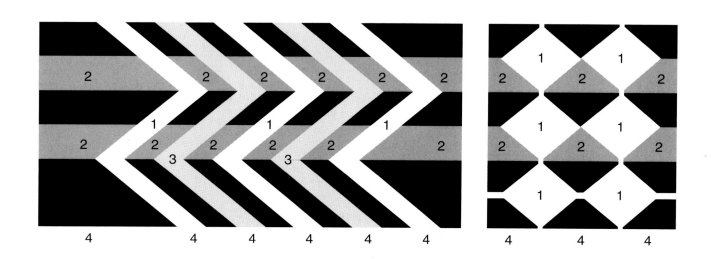

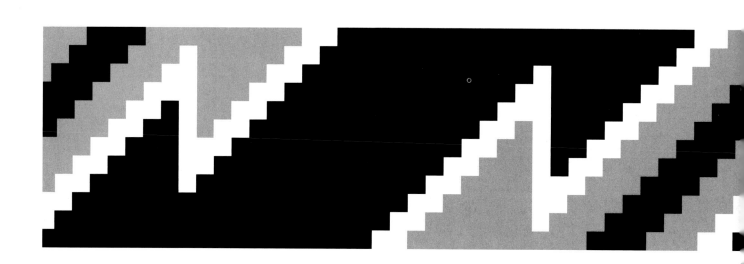

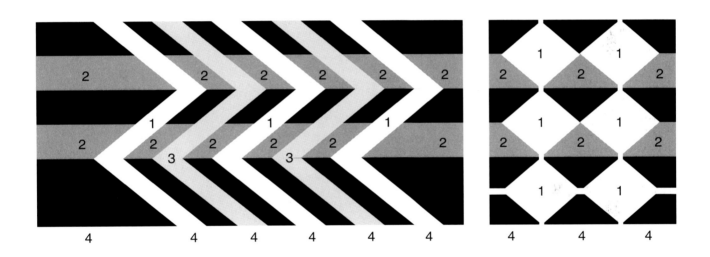

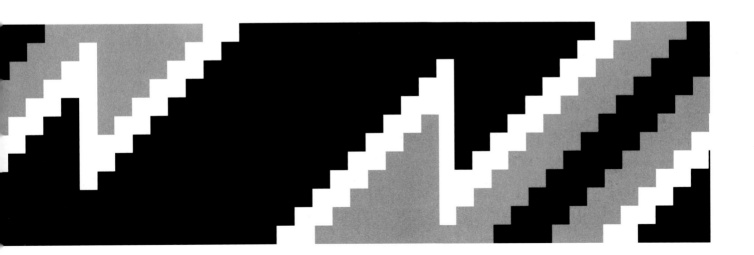

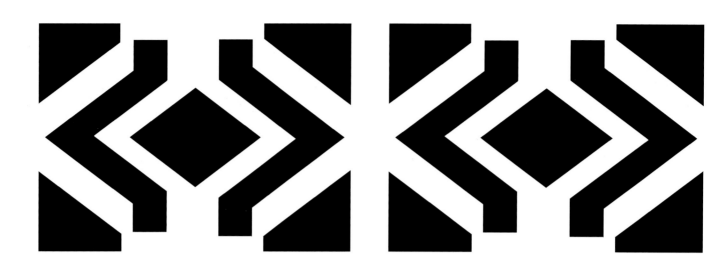

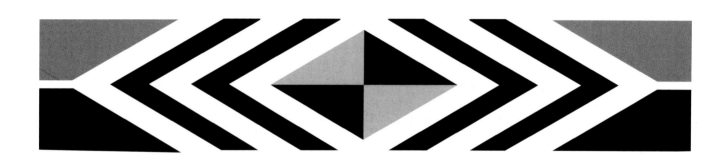

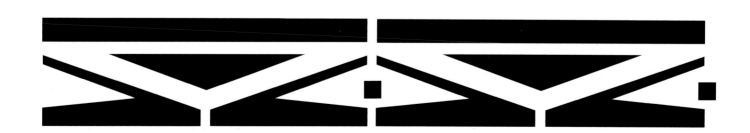

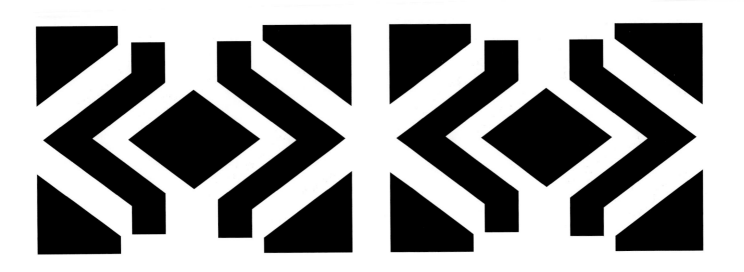

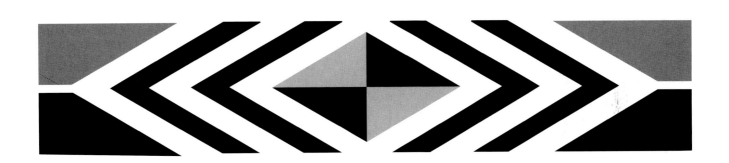

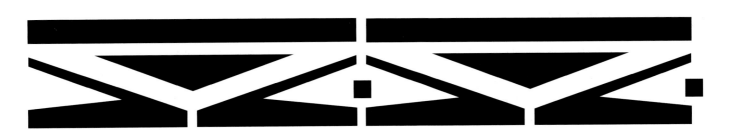

TRIBAL MOTIFS

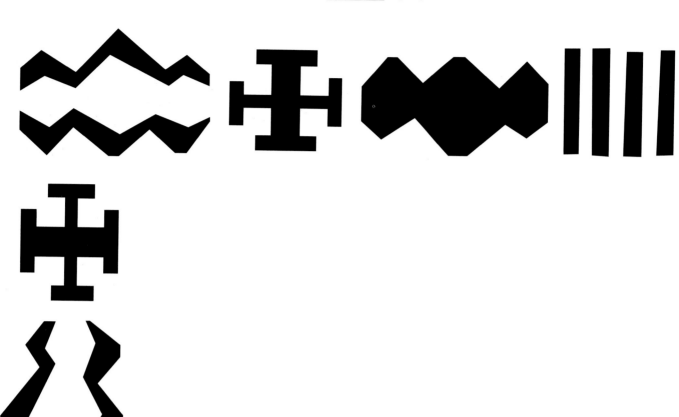

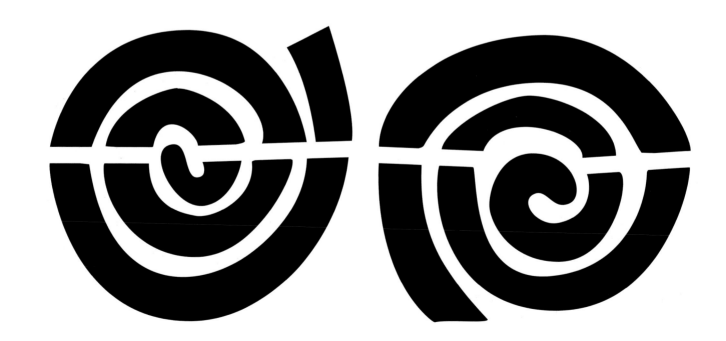

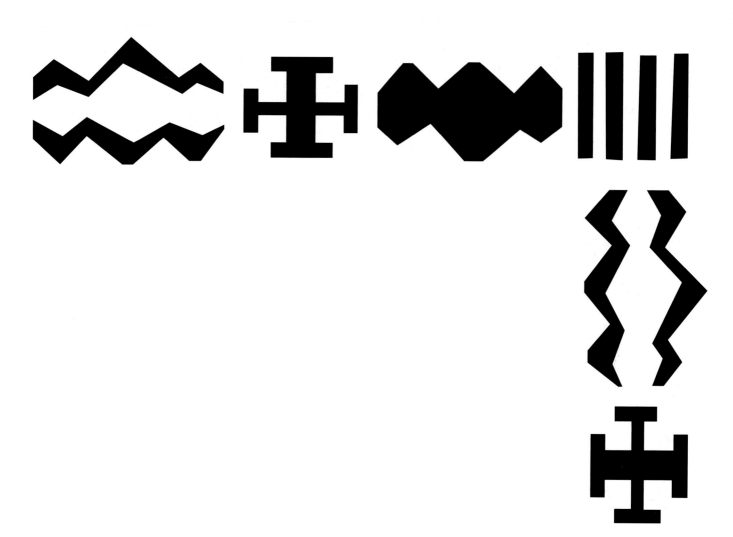

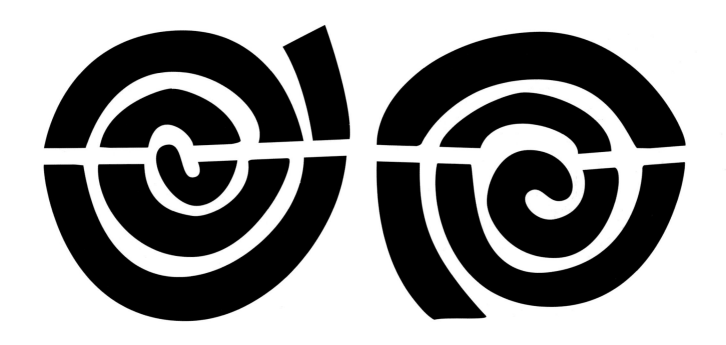

MARINE MOTIFS

THIS GROUP OF MARINE MOTIFS IS SPONTANEOUS, NAIVE, SIMPLE AND JOYFUL. THERE ARE ALL KINDS OF SEA CREATURES, FROM STARFISH TO SEA HORSES TO MERMAIDS. AND, OF COURSE, FISH! THERE ARE SHELLS, DOLPHINS, SCHOOLS OF FISH, AS WELL AS SOME MAN-MADE NAUTICAL SYMBOLS, SUCH AS ANCHORS AND SHIPS' WHEELS. THERE IS A PEACE AND CALM ABOUT MANY OF THESE IMAGES, SOMETHING THAT REMINDS US OF HOW ENORMOUS THE WORLD OF THE SEA IS AND HOW SMALL WE ARE, THAT WILL SPREAD THROUGH ANY PART OF YOUR HOME YOU USE THEM IN. THE COLOURS THAT COME FROM THE SEA WOULD SUIT THESE STENCILS BEST — BLUES, GREENS, GREYS, SILVER AND GOLD. THEY ARE PERFECT FOR BEACH HOMES, BATHROOMS, WET AREAS, BOXES, BEDS, BEACH CLOTHES, BATHING SUITS, TOWELS, LAMP SHADES, CUSHIONS. THE LIST IS ENDLESS!

MARINE MOTIFS

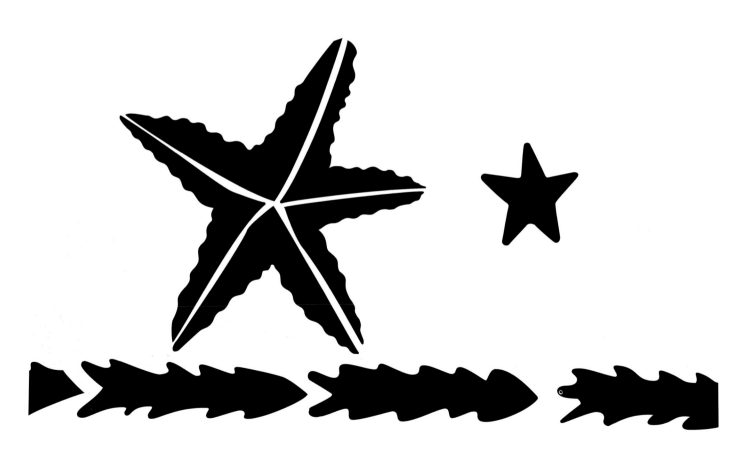

LIFESTYLE MOTIFS

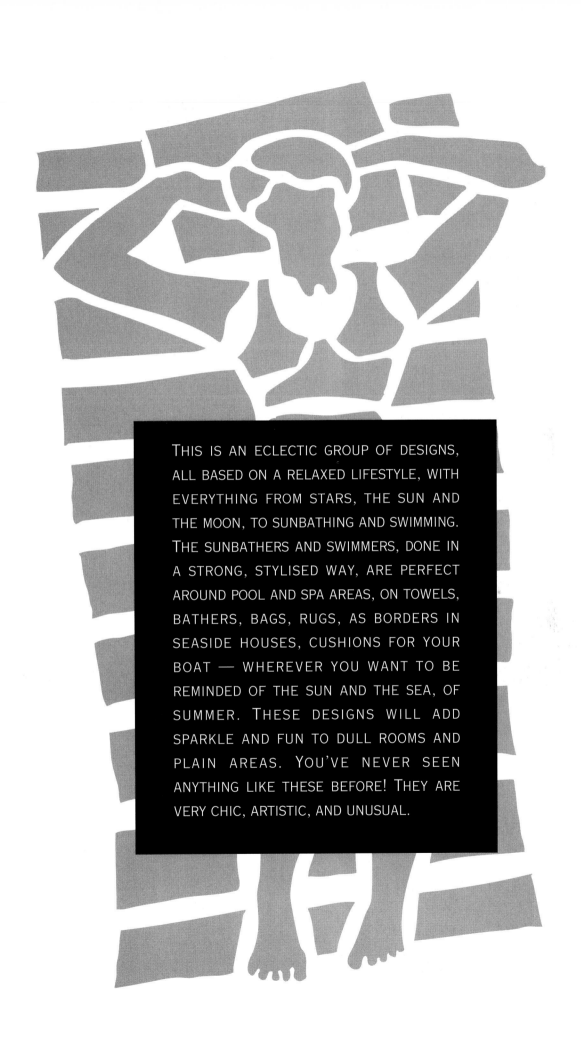

THIS IS AN ECLECTIC GROUP OF DESIGNS,
ALL BASED ON A RELAXED LIFESTYLE, WITH
EVERYTHING FROM STARS, THE SUN AND
THE MOON, TO SUNBATHING AND SWIMMING.
THE SUNBATHERS AND SWIMMERS, DONE IN
A STRONG, STYLISED WAY, ARE PERFECT
AROUND POOL AND SPA AREAS, ON TOWELS,
BATHERS, BAGS, RUGS, AS BORDERS IN
SEASIDE HOUSES, CUSHIONS FOR YOUR
BOAT — WHEREVER YOU WANT TO BE
REMINDED OF THE SUN AND THE SEA, OF
SUMMER. THESE DESIGNS WILL ADD
SPARKLE AND FUN TO DULL ROOMS AND
PLAIN AREAS. YOU'VE NEVER SEEN
ANYTHING LIKE THESE BEFORE! THEY ARE
VERY CHIC, ARTISTIC, AND UNUSUAL.

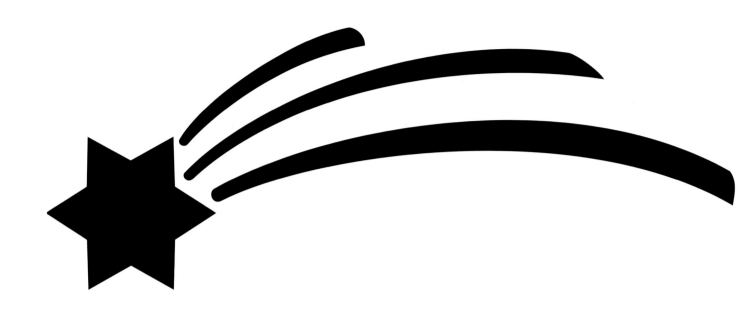

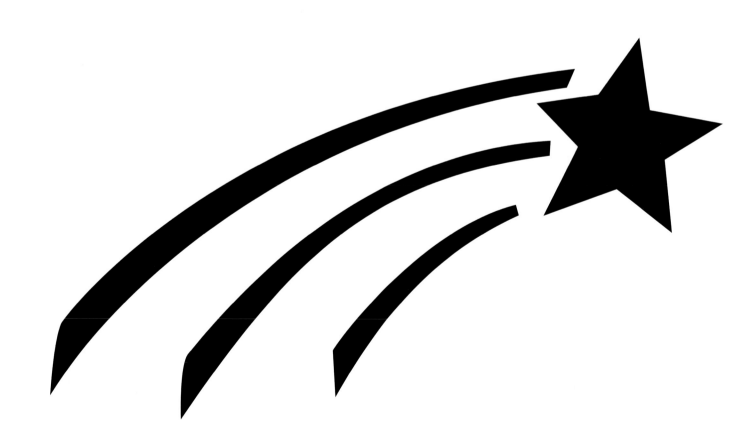

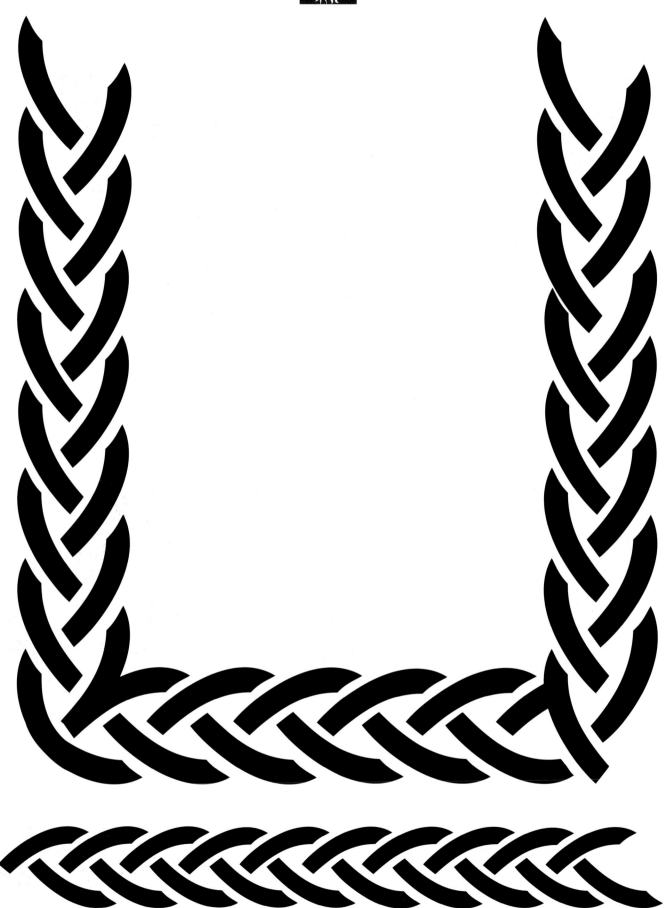

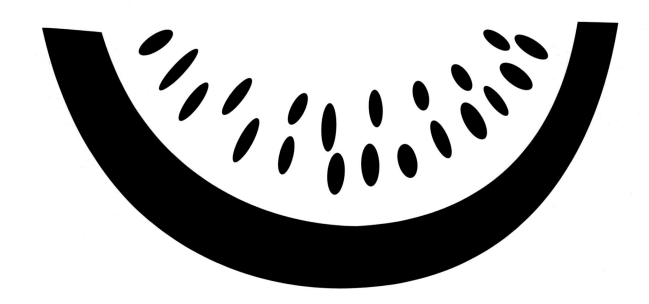

GEOMETRIC PATTERNS

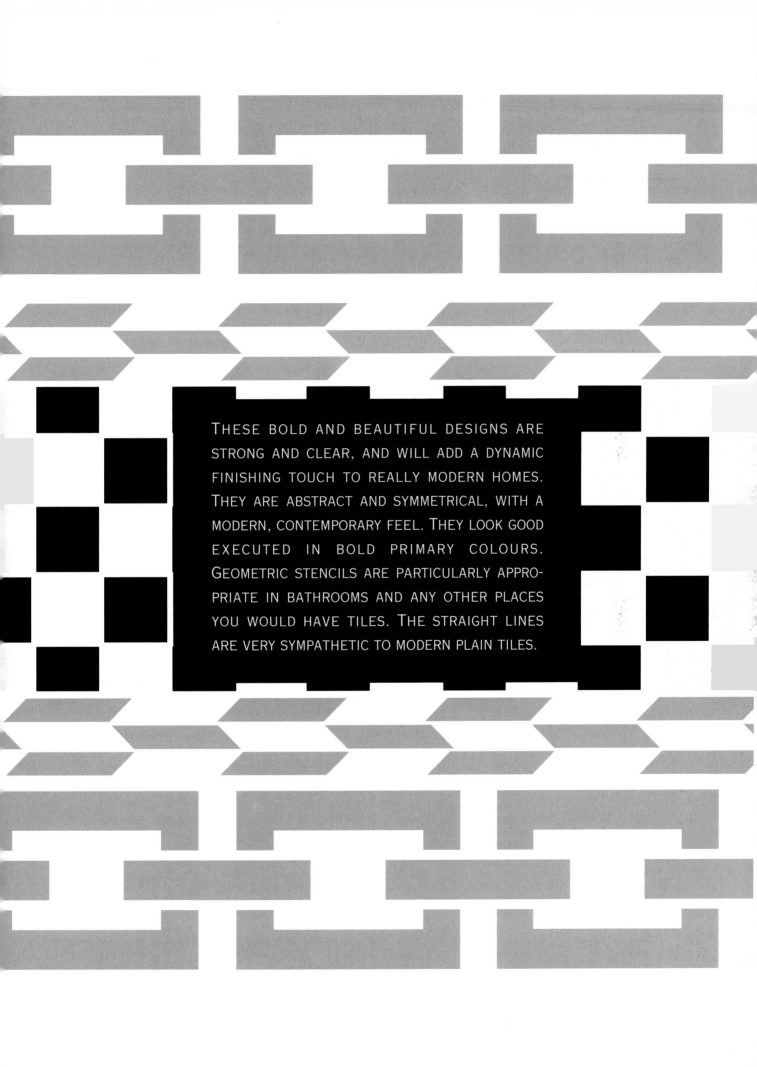

THESE BOLD AND BEAUTIFUL DESIGNS ARE STRONG AND CLEAR, AND WILL ADD A DYNAMIC FINISHING TOUCH TO REALLY MODERN HOMES. THEY ARE ABSTRACT AND SYMMETRICAL, WITH A MODERN, CONTEMPORARY FEEL. THEY LOOK GOOD EXECUTED IN BOLD PRIMARY COLOURS. GEOMETRIC STENCILS ARE PARTICULARLY APPROPRIATE IN BATHROOMS AND ANY OTHER PLACES YOU WOULD HAVE TILES. THE STRAIGHT LINES ARE VERY SYMPATHETIC TO MODERN PLAIN TILES.

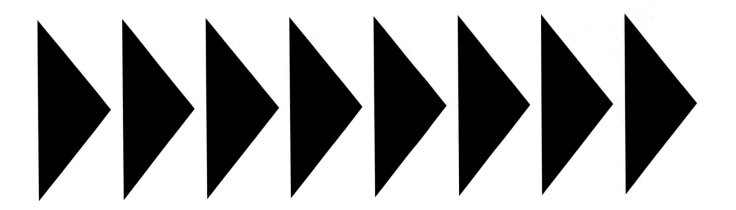

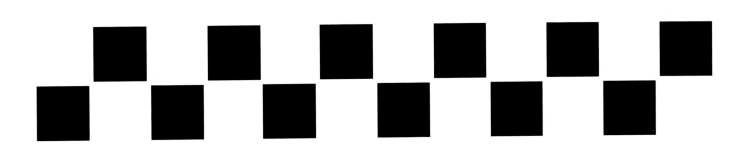

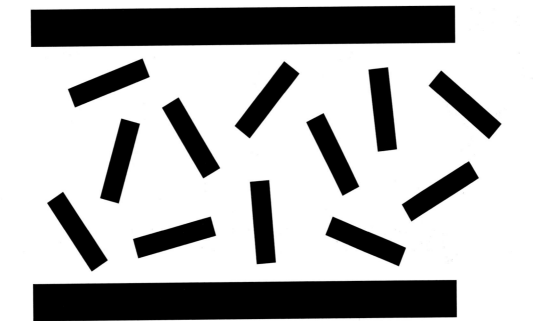

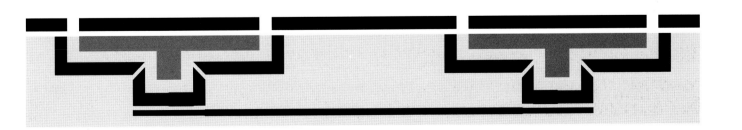

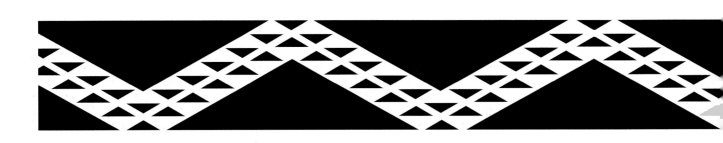

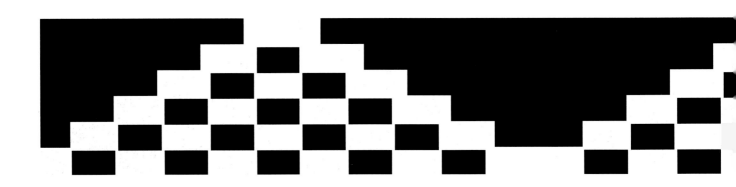

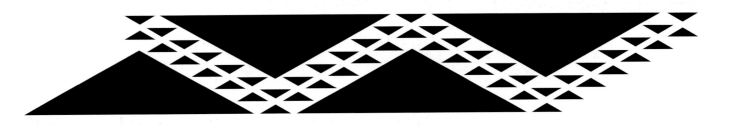

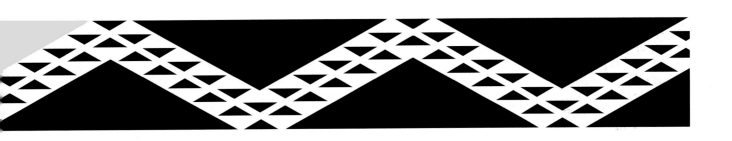

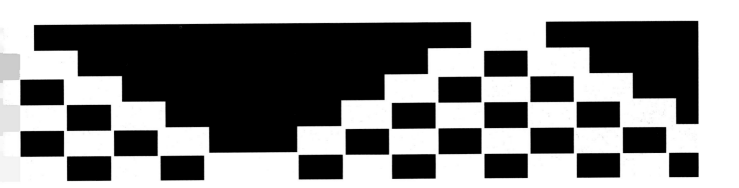

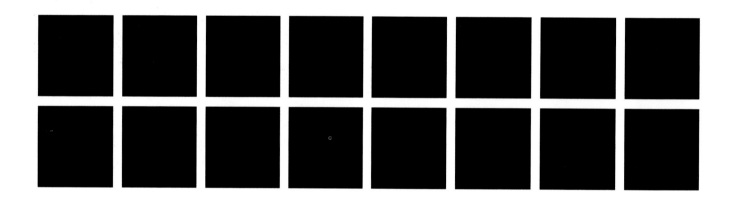